Free from poverty,
Gain prosperity

Author
Josiah Peterson

Josiah Peterson
E-mail:
Josiah@josiahpetersonministries.org

978-0-557-39402-9

Free from Poverty
Gain Prosperity
Introduction by the Author
Table of Contents

Introduction
Free from Poverty
Gain Prosperity

        I would like to introduce you to
Free from poverty, Gain prosperity. For the
following chapters you are about to read and
discover, is actual live events that was
happening in my life. Each Chapter as your
read is what I experienced personally in my
life. As God directed me and lead me to
write this book, not just for fortune or
fame, to be recognized by big names or big
churches. But to spread out the news
knowing how people can become debt free, in
their own life, and to be free from poverty.
Some many people want to be blessed, and

be prosperous but they just don't know how, and it's something new to them.

Each chapter you will read is only what God want me to put in this book. I don't want to use this book to make me popular, but to reach out to help other people who is dealing with the same issues that you are about to read, that I was dealing with.

As I was writing this book, only person that was working with me on this was God, He was the only one that helped me out of my struggles. He also used other people who I really am thankful for that has helped. If you are ready for a life changing experience in your life, your finances, your relationships, your property, your health and your personality, this book is for you.

Author
Josiah Peterson

Chapter 1

Recognizing Poverty

Why Am I always struggling? Why do I see people get blessed with more than me? Is there something I am doing wrong, or does anyone care? Why Am I always in debt? How can I get out of debt, when I keep losing my Job? What is going on in my life? What kind of spirit do I have that keeps me bound up in defeat, can't seem to get where I am going, because I am stuck to where I came from and background. Where do I go, and turn too, when all else fails. Who do I lean on? I heard of poverty, but

I doubted myself. I told myself, I don't have poverty, because I live in America. America doesn't have poverty. But that's what the enemy wanted me to believe, to keep the promises of God from me.

What is poverty? Who has poverty? Where does poverty come from? Is poverty something we see on television from another country? Or is it right in our very own life. Most of the time, people think of poverty is someone without no shelter, no food, no water, or even a place to stay to keep warm, or cool depending on the season. Also people think of poverty is having no money.

Poverty isn't just about money, but poverty can hit us in any area of our lives. Poverty is a stronghold, and a spirit. The #1 reason why we have divorces today is finances. So many people think that if you don't have finances in your marriage it won't work. But that's not what the bible says. Be careful, not to think its money that got you married. If you put money 1st in your marriage, it isn't going to work. Cause there is spirit of mamma in your relationship and you made money being your provider, and not God. It's important to have God to be 1st in everything you do. So many of us have poverty attached to us, to where the enemy, put spiritual blindness, when it comes to poverty.

What does the bible say about poverty? How can we identify poverty? Poverty is a spirit that will find a sneaky way to get around. In

Genesis 2:16-17 says, and the Lord God commanded the man saying, "Of every tree of the garden you may freely eat: But the tree of knowledge of good and evil you shall not eat. For in the day you eat of it you shall surely die."

In this passage of scripture, it could be the tithe that God said not to eat of it, because the tree belongs to him. Many times we look at our finances, like how Adam and Eve looked at the tree, for it was the serpent that went to Eve. And questioned her, made her think. Who knows what the serpent told Eve. He could have told Eve, to taste the apple, because there is plenty to go around. But that's not the case.

In the Garden of Eden, there

was only one tree that God said, not to eat of it. When Adam and Eve ate of the tree, that's when poverty began. Really people don't know they have poverty because it's in them. They are in an environment, that doesn't recognize it. Poverty is a spirit, and it's growing through our generations and ancestors. So many people don't have much,because they don't have the faith that God can give you anything you ask, pray, and believe. Faith and Doubt works against each other, God says you can have it, but you say you can't afford it. God says it's yours, but you say, I didn't pay for it.

There were times in my life, to where I was living from paycheck to paycheck, and still I was hungry, not having enough food to get by on. It seems like every car I bought, broken down, every clothes I bought, gets torned, and ripped. I was too busy trying to be like everyone else, getting what everyone else has. Little did I know, what kind of a price they paid, to get to where they are? I was in so much pride, till it almost took my life. I had to do some searching, into what I can do to change, and how I can be freed from poverty.

It's the measure of faith that you use that can get you out of the situation you are in, or to keep you there.

The bible says you can't serve two masters. You can't serve God and mammon. It's the same way with faith. You can't have faith and doubt. It's doubt that keeps your faith from working. Watch what you say when you are praying, and believing God for things.

You can't pray for something to happen in your life, and then speak against it. If you truly know, its God desire for you to have something you ask for, you already have it. Most of the promises God wants to give to us, we don't have it because it's the words we speak, and actions when we give and receive and doubting.

Sometimes to recognize what you have and don't have, you got to move from the environment you are in, move to a place where it's safe. Go on a fast, spend time with God, and through that time, God begins to work on you, work in your heart, mind, and emotions. He gets you to a place where you are at comfort, and at peace. So God can reveal some things in you that only he can change. If you allow God to change you. It's the wantness you have that produce faith. For it is faith that helps build your character.

Character is who you are when no one is looking around. You can be friendly on the outside, who are you on the inside? Do you see yourself, as what people say about you, or do you see yourself as God sees you. Do you look at your finances as the world sees it or do you see your finances as God sees it? God can help show you how to get out of poverty. Your mind and heart has to be open to what God says, and be obedient when he speaks.

Don't let your past dictate your future. I remember in my life, to where I was struggling financially, living from paycheck to paycheck. I couldn't figure why I was always broke, never have enough, always depending on loan companies, friends, and family to help me out. I begin to realize, I was leaving someone out, and it was God. I was putting my trust in all other areas, but not putting my trust of finances into God's hands. I became my own supply, When I didn't gave to God what was his, and trusting in him, not in man. God pulled his hand back from my finances, to see how long I am able to go without him; it didn't take less than 2 months to realize I needed God in my finances.

I realize it was fear and doubt

that had a grip on my pocket book. It seem liked the more I worked, the more in debt I got, I told myself what is going on. Making more than enough, but yet still saying, doesn't have enough.

God had to get me to a place, to where I couldn't do this on my own, I went running to God. Poverty had a stronghold on me, it was on me most of my life through the years growing up and when I got my first job. I really didn't know how to save money, put it into savings. It was something God had to show and reveal to me how.

Most of the words I heard people say, they couldn't afford this, don't have enough. I heard those words for so long, I believed it myself. The enemy had put the poverty spirit on me. I wanted to believe God, but doubting him. I was longing for a change, needing a fresh start. I found myself on my knees, praying out to God, asking him to free me from poverty. What is it that God want to do in me to become a better me? It was putting all my trust in him. Placing him first in my life.

No matter your background is it's not too late for you to become poverty free, and be debt free. Poverty can hit us in all areas, not just finances. And poverty can hit us when we least to expect it. When everything is going well and not producing, check your heart. Poverty can hit you in your relationships, how you take care of yourself, and how you treat others. For the words we speak have power. For man shall not live by bread alone, but by every word that comes from your mouth.

If you speak cursing, you reap cursing. If you speak lack, you reap lack. For what you sow, that you shall also reap. It's really important that you don't down size anybody's character. If someone is struggling financially, we ought not to down size them. We don't know what that person is going through. We don't know there story. If you don't want poverty in your life, there is a way to break the poverty spirit, and you can be free.

In the next coming up chapters in the book, these chapters will help you; guide you through the process, and some keys and points to where you can apply it to your life.

Chapter 2

Dealing with Poverty

In my life as I was growing up, I was in the church, listening to the teachings on tithing and offerings. I tithe and gave in offerings, it seems like all of my needs was not still getting met. Every car I bought broke down and let go back. I couldn't figure out why these things keep happening.

I couldn't help to realize it wasn't that I was tithing, which that is what God has us to give our ten percent. It was the environment I was in. I didn't know there was something wrong, until God met me at the place where he wanted me to be. At the same time I wanted to be blessed financially, and be prosperous, it seemed I couldn't get rid of the debt I was in. Loan after loan, I thought I would be out of debt, but it got me further into it instead. I was up to my knees, working my normal forty hours a week job, plus overtime, trying to make ends meet, and get out of debt. But I wasn't, my body was getting tired instead.

I knew I needed something real to happen in my life, I knew I needed something to get me out of the situation, not keeping me in. I didn't know I was dealing with a spirit of poverty until I recognized it. I begin to spend time in prayer, and communicating with God. Little by little, he began to show me the areas,

I was struggling in, and one was poverty. For Poverty had a stronghold on me, it was messing with my mind when I tithe.

As I Tithe, and believing God would get me out of debt, more bills kept on coming in. I figured out I wasn't really putting him all first.

So many times we get so caught up in the news, talking about the economy. We tend to get more of what the news says, instead what the Word says, how to get free from Poverty and staying connected to God, so through him, He can show us how to be free from poverty and gain prosperity.

As I soon started to see a breakthrough, a change to take place in my life concerning poverty. I knew I needed to something or someone to get me out of the struggle I was in. One area I needed to work on was discipline.

So many people can be prosperous; it only takes discipline and obedience.

Proverbs 11:24 NIV

One man gives freely, yet gains even more; another withholds unduly, but comes to poverty.

In this passage of scripture, it speaks on obedience. This when it comes down to where God tells you to give, and it's the actions behind your obedience determines, the outcome of prosperity in your life. For one who has more, it's so easy for him to give, if he is not stingy with his money, but to the one, who has little, withhold their whole paycheck. And don't tithe, and give, because they think that's all they have. They feel they need to hold it, don't trust God.

It's the choice of obeying, and disobeying that can get you out of poverty, or to keep you in.

Proverbs 13:18 NIV

He who ignores discipline comes to poverty and shame, but whoever heeds correction is honored.

In this passage of scripture, If God is on your case, trying to discipline you, take heed to it. But if you ignore, what God is trying to do, you only hurting yourself, causing a spirit of poverty to be on your life. But if you take the correction God gives you, and apply it to your life, God's Word promised you will be

Blessed, that God is not a man that he should lie. Because God is Truth.

Proverbs 28:22 NIV

A stingy man is eager to get rich and is unaware that poverty awaits him.

It so easy sometimes to hold to everything, and not letting go. This particular scripture isn't just talking about money. It is talking about everything pertaining to your life. Your relationships, neighborhoods, friendships, and finances. Some people are stingy when it comes to relationships. It's also the stinginess we have that awaits poverty to come into our lives.

Who is influencing you? Who's talking about you? Who cares what you have to say? When you come to the point, and realization, that God is only one you can go too, He will hold you, and guide you. Give Him your burden, For His Burden is light and his yoke is easy.

Mark 12:44 NIV

They all gave out of their wealth; but she, out of her poverty, put in everything--all she had to live on."

One key from this, to be free from poverty, is to give out of poverty. Some people give because they have it, and some give because they don't. God is looking for people who are not stingy, that he can trust, to do his will, and have a heart to give no matter how big or small the seed is.

If someone only gives 5.00 in

tithe, don't despise it, because this person gave all he or she had. Why others have $50.00 won't give a $1.00.

But this woman gave all she had and God blessed her greatly.

2 Corinthians 8:9 NIV

For you know the grace of our Lord Jesus Christ, that though he was rich, yet for your sakes he became poor, so that you through his poverty might become rich.

Before you came into the world, Jesus already bored your pain, sorrow, guilt, shame, and poverty. He gave his life for us so we won't have to suffer. Even though sometimes Life can get so difficult, that we need to put our Trust in God. He is the only friend that you can have that won't let you down. God is willing to take care of you.

While I was going through poverty I had many challenges, which I have to overcome, to receive to full blessings from God. I wanted to discover something new. I begin to search on prosperity and how to have it, and leave poverty.

I was reading in **Deuteronomy 28**. It talks about the Blessings and cursing people have. If you obey God, You reap Blessings and if you disobey God, you reap curses.

I prayed and told God to help me to obey him not to be blessed, but help to keep my trust in you.

In the next coming chapters, you are getting ready to experience a season change in your life. You will see in the next chapters how prosperity can change your life; Lot of key factors will help you to stay on course in prosperity, being free from poverty. How when to start flowing into prosperity, the next few chapters will help you to stay on course so, you won't be tempted to fall back into poverty mode.

If you are ready for a change in your relationships, finances, and every aspect of your life. Chapters 3 and up are for you. It's time to move forward, and not look back. It time's to get closer to your destiny, and then be driven away. It's time to reach your potential, to fulfill the dreams God given to you, instead of living in gloom and despair. It's time to reach for the prize that awaits us at the finish line. Are you ready for a season change in your life? Are you ready for miracles to begin to happen in your life with no turning back and nothing to return? Before you read on, and search your heart, and if there is any unforgiveness in your heart, Ask God to forgive you. Let him come in and be a part of your life and walk. And if you have hatred in your heart toward anyone, release it and let it go, don't let hatred be the only thing standing in the way of your blessing.

If you have Pride, selfishness, and idolizing. Don't let this very thing that's stands in the way of your breakthrough.

CHAPTER 3

Transitioning from Poverty to Prosperity

While giving and working are essential to experiencing "kingdom prosperity," these actions alone don't guarantee success. You must tap into the wisdom of God for true, creative thinking. Your practical use of this wisdom will produce positive results that will command the world's attention and respect—a true testimony to the value of God's kingdom.

As I begin to discover prosperity, I was still battling with the stronghold of poverty. Many times I wanted to give up, and quit, But I **knew God had something inside of** me, that he didn't bring me into this world, to give up, I realized, I am not a quitter, I am a champion, and victorious. I am a prince, I am a king. I am made to conquer.

GENESIS 1:28 "Then God blessed them, and God said to them, "Be fruitful and multiply; fill the earth and subdue it; have dominion over the fish of the sea, over the birds of the air, and over every living thing that moves on the earth."

After reading this scripture, God gave me a revelation that God said to be fruitful, that we have dominion over our circumstances. God gave us authority over the earth. I begin to put authority over my finances, and begin to speak to my finances. And I started to speak over every aspect of my life. And not letting the cares of this world hold me back or let me down.

As I was getting to a place to give up, God came into my life and showed up. I was looking for a place that I can go to and seek wisdom, knowledge and understanding. I had been in church all my life. Preachers talked about tithing. But it seems I couldn't find anyone that will go into depth of the subject. I was longing for a church home, to where I go and get medicine for my life. And get teachings and many kingdom ideas how to be blessed. I thank God for my Church home. If wasn't for God leading me there, no telling where I would be.

LEVITICUS 26:9 "For I will look on you favorably and make you fruitful, multiply you and confirm my covenant with you."

For in this passage of scripture, God is your covenant partner, not man. God is in the business of giving you favor, giving you wisdom, insight and knowledge to multiply your seed, that you sown. How to keep water the seed after you have planted it. Your job is not the source of your income; it's a seed that God gave to you to produce more seed to come into your life. God knows you need seed to plant. That's why God blesses people with side jobs, and their main 40 hour a week job, depending you are on full time, or part-time at your job. It doesn't matter how big or small the seed you get, its how you use your seed, what you do with the 1st fruits of your seed, determines the harvest that's soon awaits you.

DEUTERONOMY 8:18 "And you shall remember the Lord your God, for it is He who gives you power to get wealth, that He may establish His covenant which He swore to your fathers, as it is this day."

So many people get so caught up when God bless them with a Job, 2 or 3 years pass by, they seem to forget who got them a job. That's why is so important, not to take things God gives you for granted. God is a jealous God. Men think they have the power to create wealth, buts it's actually God's idea, but He put it in their spirit. It's so important to thank God everyday on a regular basis, so He blesses you with more.

DEUTERONOMY 29:9

"Therefore keep the words of this covenant, and do them, that you may prosper in all that you do."

One key factor for us to prosper is just do what the scripture says, that's to keep his words and obey. God wants you to prosper, and doesn't want his children to stay in black and in poverty. Some people takes longer to get back on track then others, because the road they been on has been difficult, and for some it's easy.

DEUTERONOMY 30:19 "I call heaven and earth as witnesses today against you, that I have set before you life and death, blessing and cursing; therefore choose life, that both you and your descendants may live;"

So many of us today are in circumstances that we can't blame but ourselves. For words we speak have power, they are life and death. If you want to be prosperous, you can't go around saying, you are broke. It doesn't matter how much the balance is in your checkbook, it's the balance you see in your spirit and heart.

For few years, in my checking balance, has always been in the negative, I was getting discourage, I put $300.00 in and have only $2.00 left. I wasn't complete in how to balance and budget my checkbook. So many times we blame the bank, for the mistake. But it's up to us to keep our balance in check. Be careful what you say, when you get your statements in the mail from your bank.

JOSHUA 1:7 "Only be strong and very courageous, that you may observe to do according to all the law which Moses My servant commanded you; do not turn from it to the right hand or to the left, that you may prosper wherever you go".

For in this race we are on, everyone is running at a different pace. Sometimes what we do, we compare ourselves to other runners who are well in the race, and some just started. When God signed you up for this race. There's a road, he wants you on. If someone is doing well financially. Don't try to be like them. Because you don't know the price, and the struggle they went through, to get to where they are.

Don't get caught off track with other runners, because some runners will distract you and pull you away from your blessings if you're not careful. You should prosper where ever you go. Your vision should be lifted up high, not at each other.

For some of us, the devil doesn't miss with us when we sign up to be on God's team. He waits until you get well into the race, and he sneaks his way to distract you, and plant seeds, that didn't come from God, but he made it sounded like it did. That's what he done to Eve. Get the word of God planted in you, stay rooted in the word. So you when God is speaking to you.

JOSHUA 1:8 "This Book of the

Law shall not depart from your **mouth, but you shall meditate in it** day and night, that you may observe to do according to all that is written in it. For then you will make your way prosperous, and then you will have good success.

Another key factor for us to be blessed, and prosperous, is to meditate on God's word day and night. Reading God's word should be the 1st thing you do when you rise and shine, and the last thing before you go to sleep at night. If you just do this simple thing, God is telling you how to make your way prosperous, have great success, and favor with God and man.

God sees everything, and he knows what is coming ahead. That's why important to stay in tune with him, so he can show you, and help you along the way.

For we are the generation Paul spoke of in **2 Timothy 3:1:** "This know also, that in the last days perilous times shall come." Satan has been increasing his attacks against Believers in these last days. His goal is to cause us to cave in and quit before we experience a breakthrough, and he's using insufficiency to accomplish his task. However, you don't have to be a victim of this vicious tactic.

The key to overcoming insufficiency in your life is to believe in and stand firmly on God's Word, which declares that the righteous (those in right—standing with God) will be upheld. **Psalm 37:18, 19** says,

"The LORD knoweth the days of the upright: and their inheritance shall be forever. They shall not be ashamed in the evil time: and in the days of famine they shall be satisfied." Confession plays a key role in helping you reach the good life God has for you. Freedom from insufficiency is possible if you: (1) sow financial seed as God directs and (2) use your mouth to speak the Word over your life

In **Luke 6:38**, Jesus says, "Give, and it shall be given unto you; good measure, pressed down, and shaken together, and running over, shall men give into your bosom. For with the same measure that ye mete withal it shall be measured to you again." You must continue to obey God in your giving, even when your resources are wearing thin. Why? You reap what you sow (**Galatians 6:7—9**). When you sow as God directs, you position yourself to reap increase.

The widow at Zarephath is a perfect example of someone who stayed on the giving side of life even when her resources had run out. She was down to her last meal when Elijah asked her to prepare a cake for him (**1 Kings 17:13**). When she did, she experienced increase in her life. Not only did her resources multiply, but her son was also brought back to life! A seed will definitely meet any need you have.

Keep in mind the power of words (**Proverbs 18:21**). Words are seeds. Whatever you speak will come back to you in the form of positive or negative manifestations. It's easy to become weary and give up when the pressure is on. But if you continue to speak positive, faith—filled words over your situation, you will see breakthrough. Don't allow the devil to oppress you with the cares of life. God is Faithful to pull you through!

Chapter 4

Accepting Prosperity

You don't have to be subject to the stress of lack because you have access to Jesus' peace! Have confidence that He will provide your every need. **John 14:27** says, "Peace I leave with you, my peace I give unto you: not as the world gives, give I unto you. Let not your heart be troubled, neither let it be afraid." Tap into this supernatural peace and rest confidently, knowing you can triumph over the devil every time!

Many people today live from paycheck to paycheck, struggling to make ends meet. That is not truly

living; it is merely surviving.
Tragically, many of the people who live this way are born-again Believers. But that's not the way God intended for our lives to be. Jesus said in **John 10:10**, "The thief cometh not, but for to steal, and to kill, and to destroy: I am come that they might have life, and that they might have it more abundantly." Yet far too many Christians know little or nothing of the abundant life that Jesus came to bring. And many who do find it hard to believe that abundance is God's desire for them.

If you are a Believer and you want to receive the abundant life, you can do so by abiding in the anointing. "But ye have an unction [anointing] from the Holy One, and ye know all things...and this is the promise that he hath promised us, even eternal life" (**1 John 2:20, 25**). The word **unction** comes from a Greek word that means "to smear or anoint with an ointment." The purpose of this function is to enable you to know all the things you need to know so that you can accomplish whatever it is you need to do.

The entire human race can tap into the anointing through Jesus Christ and put an end to life's struggles. You can experience breakthrough in every area of your life, including your finances! And you don't have to look on the outside for something you already have on the inside. You have abundance, millionaire status, a potentially prosperous idea, a million-dollar revelation or a corporation on the inside of you! For example, if you are anointed to sew beautiful garments, seek God for wisdom to discover how you can profit from this empowerment. You don't have to spend another day struggling to pay your bills or trying to accumulate wealth. Instead, allow the anointing to enhance your talents, skills and abilities.

The anointing is not given just to provide miraculous manifestations in church services. Although it will bring miracles when Believers get together, that is not its primary purpose. With the anointing, you can break through all human limitations. Instead of being limited by your natural ability, you operate in supernatural power. In other words, the anointing equips you to have a quality of life that is far above and beyond anything you would normally experience on your own. It is God's assurance that you will always prosper regardless of the circumstances.

Deuteronomy 8:18 says, "But thou shall remember the Lord thy God: for it is he that gives thee power to get wealth...." The word "**power**" simply means the ability to get results. The way you release power is by tapping into the anointing God has placed on your life. Not only does it remove burdens and destroy yokes (**Isaiah 10:27**), but it also births power, wisdom, understanding, counsel, might, knowledge and fear of the Lord (**Isaiah 11:2**). When these seven facets of the anointing are operating in your life, nothing can prevent you from entering your wealthy place!

Chapter 5

Walking in Prosperity

Did you know that you have the ability to overcome every negative situation that you face? Battles are a part of life, and you must be equipped by God with might in order to win them. The act of winning the battle is called conquest. It is the act of conquering, and is yours by faith. As a Believer, you have been made a conqueror through Jesus, and you can trust that He will enable you to get the victory.

The Word of God declares that you are more than a conqueror through Jesus Christ (**Romans 8:37**).

Being more than a conqueror means
that the victory God wants to give you
will far exceed your expectations. The
challenge that most Christians have is
resisting the temptation to try and do
things in their own abilities. They
forget that it is through Him that
they are able to conquer debt, lack
and financial hardship.

One of the many challenging battles
that people face is in the area of
their finances. When the bills are
piling up and creditors are calling your
house nonstop, it can be difficult to
feel as if you have the power to
overcome lack. However, how you feel
has nothing to do with what God can
do. By tapping into *His* supernatural
power, you can be victorious over what
appears to be a lack of financial

provision.

Though your situation may seem impossible, you have the assurance of knowing that nothing is too hard for God. When you realize that you have the ability to consistently win battles, you won't tolerate living from paycheck to paycheck and going in debt to have your needs met. Take authority over lack in the name of Jesus and ask God to give you wisdom and strategies to use.

Many times, particularly where finances are concerned, Christians are quick to work on the spiritual aspects of their breakthroughs such as prayer, making faith confessions from the Word and giving tithes and offerings, but they fail to do the natural part. Doing one without the other won't get you anywhere.

In looking at your financial profile, it is important to determine where you need to make adjustments in your financial decisions. When you are responsible with what God has already given you, He will empower you to have more. For example, spending beyond your means is not going to help you overcome debt and lack but will only lead you further into a financial hole. Using credit cards all the time and buying things that you know you can't afford are all factors in the poverty equation. If you continue being irresponsible with your money, you will continue to lack the finances you need to bless others and take care of yourself. However, by doing your part in the natural, along with the spiritual aspect from the Word, you will never run out. In fact, God will increase you at every turn. Conquerors are made by God. When His supernatural ability gets on you, you can conquer anything. **First Samuel 16:13** says, "Then Samuel took the horn of oil, and anointed him [David] in the midst of his brethren: and the Spirit of the Lord came upon David from that day forward..." Just as David was, you are anointed to be victorious over lack. Don't let the devil bog you down with what looks like an impossible situation. Receive the ability to overcome. God will bring you out every time.

Everyday we are bombarded with debt—canceling methods. TV, radio, newspapers, and magazines all offer a host of ways to quickly eliminate debt; however, the best way to eliminate debt is God's way. Yes, God is a debt—canceling God! This is why the Believer is better equipped than those who don't know the Lord. God loves you, and He does not want you to carry the burden of debt. Of course, having debt is not a sin; however, it's not God's best. Debt has wreaked havoc in many lives. It can be linked to divorce and other failed relationships, and it causes stress, which can lead to serious health problems.

God is able to help you live a debt—free life. In **2 Kings 6**, a man was cutting down a tree, when his ax head fell into the water. The man shouted "... Alas, master! For it was borrowed"

(**2 Kings 6:5**). To keep the man out of debt, God performed a miracle and made the ax head swim. God would not waste His power if He didn't think canceling this man's debt was indeed necessary. God wanted this man released from debt, so He performed a miracle on his behalf; and He will do the same for you! Although, God is a debt—canceling God, it's important to understand that this doesn't mean He will cancel everyone's debt in the same manner.

Chapter 6

You are prosperous

There are spiritual and practical laws that govern debt cancellation. God has His part, and we have ours. For example, we must pay our bills on time, and be people of integrity and character who are diligent, hard workers, not swindlers. We also have to avoid sin, and obey God's Word; doing this will ensure that God is on our side. Sin will separate you from God, and when you are in debt, you cannot afford to be separated from God!

God is merciful, and always ready to help you end the destructive cycle of debt. However, He won't do all the work. You must make a quality decision to apply the practical principles that govern debt cancellation. For example, avoid being involved in hyper consumption. God expects you to be a good steward, and manage your money wisely. Develop a budget. This will not only help you manage your money better, it will also help you pay your bills, save money, and track your spending down to the dollar. These are some practical steps that will help you get out of debt God's way.

Tithing is a spiritual principle you must apply if you expect to see God's supernatural blessing on your finances. **Malachi 3** describes how the windows of Heaven will open up and pour you out a blessing when you bring your tithes into God's house. Once you have the blessing, or an empowerment to prosper, debt can't wreak havoc in your life.

Many years ago, God revealed to me that Satan wants Christians to remain heavily burdened by debt because it hinders their ability to finance the Kingdom of God. Think about it, if all your money is tied into bills, it will be difficult to support the church!

God wants you out of debt, so declare war on debt starting today! Make a quality decision to get out of debt God's way by applying the spiritual and practical laws necessary for supernatural debt cancellation. Use the Word of God as a weapon against the spirit of debt, and refuse to be weighed down by debt another day.

Everyone wants to live the good life, but not everyone is willing to do what is necessary to reach that destination. Often when we talk about prosperity, we fail to include a vital component of achieving it—obedience. When you aren't obedient to God and His Word, you make it difficult to receive the manifestation of His blessings. Your heavenly Father is always looking for those who are willing to yield to His every instruction, even if they don't understand why He is telling them to do a particular thing. Though it may be challenging at times, when you cultivate obedience in your life, you open yourself up to receive every promise God has made in His Word.

Obedience is defined as the act or practice of obeying; being dutiful or submissive and in compliance. We practice obedience in so many areas of our lives, but often we ignore the most important person whom we are to obey—God. We tend to say it is difficult to obey God's Word and follow His commandments, but we obey the stop light that tells us to halt at an intersection! We observe speed limits and obey the law that says we must pay for goods and services rendered, but too often we fail to be in compliance with God and His rules for our lives.

Please understand God doesn't want you to obey Him because He is trying to be mean, harsh and make your life difficult or burdensome. His Word is a book of guidelines born out of love and designed to bring you to a place of joy, abundance, lasting success and fulfillment. Obedience connects you to every dream, vision, provision and promise you can imagine. You can choose how great a life you experience by choosing how much of God's Word you will obey. The choice is yours. God outlined the results of obedience in **Deuteronomy 30:15, 16** (The Amplified Bible). It says:

See, I have set before you this day life and good, and death and evil. [If you obey the commandments of the Lord your God which] I command you today, to love the Lord your God, to walk in His ways, and to keep His commandments and His statutes and His ordinances, then you shall live and multiply, and the Lord your God will bless you...

The key to connecting to the blessing of God, which empowers you to prosper in life, is obedience. Without it, you simply won't reach and fulfill your goal of living the good life.

Obedience sets you apart from the crowd. The world is full of people who have made their own rules and follow their own standards that don't line up with God's Word. As a result, they experience the negative outcomes of disobeying God. But when you obey God, you demonstrate that you belong to Him. **Exodus 19:5** says, "Now therefore, if ye will obey my voice indeed, and keep my covenant, then ye shall be a peculiar treasure unto me above all people: for all the earth is mine."

At times it may be challenging to go against the grain and obey God in the midst of the world's system which disregards what He says. You may even have family members and loved ones whose lifestyles contradict the Bible. Your obedience in the midst of their behavior makes you a shining light and example to them. When the blessings of God begin to show up in your life, they'll want an explanation as to how and why good things are happening for you. You'll be able to witness the love of God to them and let them know that obeying His Word pays off.

The bottom line is that it is wise

and in your best interest to obey God. **Isaiah 1:19** says that if you are willing and obedient, you will eat the good of the land. That means abundance! From your finances to your health, obedience is the key to living a prosperous life. Whatever God tells you to do, do it!

Some people don't understand the difference between true prosperity and false prosperity. They believe that in order to be prosperous, a person must have an abundance of money and material goods. While money is a part of the prosperity equation, it is not the whole thing. When we see the word "rich" in the Bible, it refers to wholeness, with nothing missing or broken in your life.

Think of prosperity as a pie with many slices, each one standing for an aspect of God's promises—healing, money, deliverance, a sound mind, a happy marriage, etc. Satan stole the pieces of the pie when Adam disobeyed God in the Garden of Eden, but Jesus came to the earth to restore the prosperity pie. True prosperity is having completeness in every area of your life, from your finances to your relationships with others. It is part of the abundant life that God has designed for every Believer.

False prosperity, on the other hand, is often born out of a need for instant gratification. It is having the appearance of prosperity, without the true substance of it. Society teaches us that it is acceptable to purchase luxury items we can't afford on credit, buy now and pay later and if it feels good, do it. This mentality promotes reckless spending that while on the outside may cause a person to look prosperous, is really destroying them. Accumulating debt and buying things on credit is not God's best for your life. He wants you to be a lender and not a borrower because borrowing from others puts you in the position of being the servant of debt. **Romans 13:8** says we should owe no man anything but love. When God blesses people with wealth he adds no sorrow with it (**Proverbs 10:22**).

We should want God's best in every area of our lives, especially our finances. After all, it is His will for

our lives. **Ecclesiastes 5:19, 20** says
"...It is a good thing to receive wealth
from God and the good health to
enjoy it. To enjoy your work and
accept your lot in life—that is indeed
a gift from God. People who do this
rarely look with sorrow on the past,
for God has given them reasons for
joy" (The New Living Translation).
Part of God's plan for prosperity
means enjoying the fruit of your labor
and being able to live a financially
sound life.

Many times Believers feel God
has left them when they don't
experience financial success but God
promises to provide for us in every
area. He will prosper you in your
finances if you release your faith and
stand on His Word.

As in any covenant relationship, you have a part in achieving true prosperity. Your job is to walk in love and pursue your Heavenly Father and His Kingdom first, not money or material things (**Matthew 6:33**). You must also make the Word of God your final authority in life. In doing so, you position yourself for increase.

The Bible says it is impossible to serve God and money. **Matthew 6:24** says, "No one can serve two masters; for either he will hate the one and love the other, or he will stand by and be devoted to the one and despise and be against the other. You cannot serve God and mammon [deceitful riches, money, possessions, or what is trusted in]" (The Amplified Bible). While money makes an excellent servant, it makes a terrible master.

People serve money when their pursuit of it determines every decision they make. This is called materialism; or having a wrong relationship with material things. When you become consumed with thoughts of constantly having more and acquiring more material wealth so that you can indulge it on yourself, or when you get your security from money and material goods, you are serving money. This is wrong.

True prosperity comes from having a solid relationship with the Lord and trusting Him to meet your every need as well as fulfill the desires He places in your heart. He also wants you to have more than enough to share with others. As you walk in obedience to His Word, He will bless you with these things and more. When you are operating in the overflow in every area of your life, you are operating in true prosperity, and are fulfilling His plan for you to be a blessing to others.

Many people think fear is a normal and acceptable part of life. I've even heard some people say, "There's nothing wrong with having just a little fear." Nothing could be further from the truth. Fear is anything but normal. From a natural perspective, fear is associated with simply being afraid. But spiritually speaking, fear is actually twisted faith. It is having faith in the devil and what he can do, rather than having faith in God and His Word.

Fear as a spirit that doesn't come from God (**2 Timothy 1:7**). To live in fear sets you up for disaster because just like faith will connect you to the promises of God, fear will connect you to the things you fear. When you operate from a position of fear, you actually position yourself to receive the very things you are afraid of.

In examining fear and its impact on your life, it is important to consider words and their creative power. Words are spiritual containers that carry either faith or fear. Words of faith are encouraging, hopeful and in line with the Word of God. On the other hand, words of fear are full of doubt, unbelief, dread and despair. Fear-filled words go against what God has said in His Word and will cancel out the good things that He has planned for your life.

It is critical that you align your words with the Word if you want to override the spirit of fear when it tries to attack you. Faith-filled words empower God to move on your behalf.

Fear is designed to stop you from experiencing all that God has promised you in His Word, but the good news is that He has already delivered you from it. If you are in relationship with God, you don't have to be ruled by any type of fear. **Hebrews 2:14, 15** says, "Forasmuch then as the children are partakers of flesh and blood, he also himself likewise took part of the same; that through death he might destroy him that had the power of death, that is, the devil; and deliver them who through fear of death were all their lifetime subject to bondage." Fear is the primary tool Satan uses to destroy people's lives. But the ability of the enemy has been annihilated by Jesus Christ. You are no longer subject to fear.

There is a way to flush fear out of your life if you find yourself struggling with it. The key is walking in the love of God and allowing His love to mature in your life. **First John 4:18** says, "There is no fear in love; but perfect love casteth out fear: because fear hath torment. He that feared is not made perfect in love." Every time you walk in love toward others (**1 Corinthians 13**) and maintain a consciousness of God's love for you, you kick fear out.

Once you get the fear out of your life, your faith "receiver" will be free and clear of all interference. You will then be able to believe God for His promises without hindrances. Allowing the love of God to rise in you will support your faith and position you to receive the blessings of God— healing, deliverance, safety, provision and financial increase.

In the midst of life's trials, refuse fear. I don't care what is going on around you. Resist fear with everything in you. Confess the Word of God over your situation until you begin to see things change. Stand firm on the Scriptures which will help to build your faith. Begin to praise God for what He has already done for you. Have confidence in God and His Word and don't let fear contaminate your faith and let joy be a part of your life.

By the time you reach to this part of this book, you are beginning to you realize that you are a winner, you are an over comer, you are debt free; you are free from the bondages of debt and poverty. That from this moment on you are prosperous. No matter what is going on around you, don't let the devil fool you. Stay on top of your game, that you know when to play the cards right, when he wants to play.

Put the word of God over every seed you plant, and water the seed every day, by mediating on God's and prayer. If you had made mistakes in your area of giving, ask God to forgive you, and start over. Start fresh. Work your way to the top of the ladder. It takes practice, discipline, and obedience to maintain this prosperous walk and journey.

CHAPTER 7

Message from the Author

As in closing of the book, "Free from Poverty, Gain Prosperity," I like to leave a message with you, to apply it to your everyday life, and key pointers and strategies to help you to stay on this course, not to drift back into poverty again, and say good bye to debt once and for all.

God wants you to enjoy kingdom prosperity.

There are seven actions required to experience kingdom prosperity: **giving, working, thinking, trusting, waiting, talking and**

thanking. Mere giving alone is not enough for you to experience kingdom prosperity; it only connects you to, or makes available to you, God's blessing.

Although it is necessary to work, it is not sufficiency enough for you to experience kingdom prosperity; it only provides you with a channel through which the blessing can flow. Creative work guarantees productivity, which guarantees wealth.

Wealth is the offspring of wisdom (Proverbs 3:13-16, *AMP*).

You must never become so "overly spiritual" that you neglect the natural aspects of prospering in the things of God; that's where the third action of kingdom prosperity comes in—thinking. Thinking is "the ability to coordinate thoughts productively for increased output."

Reasoning makes you rich. You must be sound, or highly productive, in your thinking (**Ephesians 1:17-18**, *AMP*).

Think to create something productive that will make living great.

Wise work begets wealth. (Example): A man who is laboring without seeing results will grow weary of the work; eventually, he'll quit working. He knows what to do but doesn't know how to do it—he lacks direction (**Ecclesiastes 10:15**). Knowing what to do without knowing how to do something creates a problem.

The wisdom of knowing how to do a thing is what guarantees results. Work smarter, not just harder.

Abundance is deposited within you and must be drawn out. All of the wealth in the universe came as a result of wisdom (**Psalm 104:24**).

Engage wisdom.

Just as a car's gears must be engaged to drive it, you must engage God's Word for it to benefit your life. Don't associate with pessimistic "buzzards;" instead, associate with dreamers. Creative thinking brought Joseph out of slavery; it will deliver you out of bondage to lack, debt, sickness and any other aspect of the curse.

Every throne is created by wisdom; the throne of your life must be created.

Creative wisdom is the principal thing needed to create what does not yet exist (**Proverbs 4:7**).

Wisdom is an anointing—the power of God that removes burdens and destroys yokes (**1 Corinthians 1:24**).

New thoughts can produce new things; therefore, command the world's attention and respect through creative thinking. Don't take the credit for the wisdom that God gives you. Be courageous and lives in free so that you can step out on what God reveals to you.

You cannot move toward prosperity without the seed of God's Word first entering your life. The Word provides the light that is needed to break the chains of poverty. Your first concern must be the prosperity of your soul, which determines your position in life. When your soul is prospering, you will see results (tangible materials). God's Word is your foundation for prosperity and the water that your financial seeds need in order to grow.

Power is a necessary element to move you from one place in your life to another **(Deuteronomy 8:17-18)**...

God has given you power to get wealth. You must *arise*, or "change your posture and position," in order for prosperity to manifest itself in your life **(Isaiah 60:1)**.

Without light--the light of God's Word--you will stay the same. If you are born again, you are the seed of Abraham and have a right to the promises of God. Prosperity is born out of a covenant God made with His words—the words found in the Bible **(Joshua 1:8).**

God takes pleasure in your prosperity because He is magnified in it **(Psalm 35:27).** Society has reduced prosperity to money, but God is interested in total life prosperity, which includes, but is not limited to, money.

Total life prosperity is "shalom"—continual well being and success. Prosperity can't be bad if God takes pleasure in it. Jesus restored all of the pieces of the "prosperity pie" that the Devil stole.

Jesus came to preach the Gospel to the poor—those who were lacking something. It is good to give to the poor; however, you must remember to preach the Gospel to them as well (**Matthew 11:4-5**). It is possible to be rich in material assets and poor in other areas of your life (**Revelation 3:17**).

Although a person may be financially wealthy, he or she may be lacking meaningful relationships or be dying of cancer. Total life prosperity begins in the soul (**3 John 2**). The prosperity of your soul must be your first priority because it determines your position in life. Soul prosperity comes from the revelation of God's Word. If you are "down on your luck," it is not because of luck, but because you are lacking the light of God's Word.

It is impossible for you not to prosper when the Word is operational in your heart. The Word of God is your highway to the world of wealth (**Job 22:21-22**). If you take the seed of God's Word and put it in your heart, then wealth and riches will be in your house (**Psalm 112:1-3**). Seek out people who are sent with the message of prosperity to break the poverty chain.

The seed of God's Word controls the outcome of your endeavors in the kingdom of God.

Prosperity is born out of truth-- if you don't love truth, you'll never be free from trials (**Psalm 45:3-4**). Wisdom and light lead to mighty works (**Matthew 13:54**). Light comes when revelation knowledge of the Word enters your heart. The Word of God is the all-controlling seed (**Luke**

8:11). Every "Word seed" has a harvest time.

To prosper in any area, you have to have revelation knowledge of that particular area. God doesn't prosper you on the basis of your money seed, but on the basis of the light you have inside of you. When the Word is operational in your life, it causes your money seed to increase. Until the Word seed is in place, there is no future for your money seed. God's Word is your foundation for prosperity.

A sturdy foundation is necessary to sustain any kingdom principle (**Psalm 11:3**).Prosperity can't be established without the proper foundation. Once the Church has a strong foundation, all nations will flow to it (**Isaiah 2:2**).God will build up the Church to its highest point, then He will appear in His glory (**Psalm 102:16**).

Part of building a strong foundation is living a righteous life (**Isaiah 3:10**). If the Devil can successfully destroy the foundation of God's Word in your life, he can see you fail over and over again.

God has not called His children to remain in the dark.

As a born-again Christian, it has been given to you to know the mysteries of the kingdom of God (**Mark 4:11**). God has knowledge that will bring results in your life. The common denominator for your escape from problematic situations is revelation from God. The natural, carnal-minded man is on the outside of revelation knowledge (**1 Corinthians 2:14**). He is "without" God or the knowledge of God.

God will show His secrets to those who fear Him (**Psalm 25:14**). When you walk in the fear of the Lord, you allow God to do wonderful things in your life. Walking in the fear of God means hating evil. What you do every day is what you develop; therefore learn to develop an iniquity-free lifestyle. Accept responsibility for where you are. Don't be like a dog and "return to your vomit," or return to the way you did things when you were unsaved (**2 Peter 2:20-22; Proverbs 26:11; Revelation 22:15**). God can't prosper a person who is living like a dog. Jesus' advice to dogs is to depart from iniquity. God wants to convict you of sin so that you will stop. You become a candidate for kingdom prosperity when you live a consecrated life.

Prosperity is not just about money. Christians need to know that there is total life prosperity, or wholeness and continuous well-being for every area of their lives. To experience total life prosperity, you must first understand how it works. Consecration is a key element of this kind of prosperity.

Your giving establishes a connection to the blessing (empowerment to prosper) while your work provides the channel through which the blessing flows to you. You will not be a beneficiary of the blessing if you are unemployed.

Your words determine the course of your life. If you are not saying anything, you are not creating anything. Create your world by confessing God's Word. If you believe something, you will speak it aloud. Confession confirms what you say you believe in your heart and releases the faith for what you believe to come to pass in your life.

Father God we thank you for your Word that you have established in this book. Lord I pray that this book has helped someone out today, that they will start shining like a dove and soar like an eagle.

Father God we thank you for patience and kindness upon us even though we tend to make mistakes and fall behind. From this moment on Lord, We put everything into your hands that your guidance is upon our lives, churches, families, friends, and our countries.

Lord I thank you for giving me this ability to write this book for the people. And to touch their hearts, souls, and minds.

In Jesus Name we pray. Amen

Notes

Notes

Notes

Notes

www.ingramcontent.com/pod-product-compliance
Lightning Source LLC
Chambersburg PA
CBHW031253280526
45784CB00004B/1840